The balance of nature is both a subtle and complex thing. Ever since Man started to farm and hunt, he has disturbed it and turned it to his own advantage. The present scale of that disturbance makes it imperative that we understand more about the balance and take steps to restore it where possible. Here is a simple approach to Ecology with clear illustrations to emphasise and extend each point.

Nature's Roundabout

an introduction to Ecology

by Patrick Armstrong BSc MA PhD

illustrated by
David Palmer

Ladybird Books Loughborough

WHAT IS ECOLOGY? COMMUNITIES
OF ANIMALS AND PLANTS

The word *ecology* comes from two Greek words
meaning 'home' and 'science'; thus ecology is the
scientific study of animals and plants in their homes or
natural habitats. Plants and animals live together in
communities: an oak wood, a stream, an area of
heathland or a rock-pool by the sea-shore are all
examples of ecological communities.

Ecology deals with the relationships, or links, between
the various animals and plants that live in such a
community or habitat. It is also concerned with the way
in which the various creatures living in any habitat are
affected by such things as the soil, the climate and man's
activities. Many dozens of types of plants and animals
live together in a hedgerow community. If the hedge
itself is of hawthorn its leaves will provide food in

4 *Field Mouse*

Redwing

Fieldfare

Fieldfare

summer for many caterpillars, and these in turn will be
eaten by small birds such as blackcaps, who use the
protection provided by the hedgerow for their nests.
Spiders may spin their webs between the outer twigs of
the hedge. In autumn and early winter the 'haws' are
eaten by birds such as thrushes, fieldfares and redwings.
Mice eat the stones of the hawthorn fruit, sometimes
hoarding them in old birds' nests. Sometimes hedges are
planted along the crest of a low bank. Often a ditch
runs along the base of a hedge. In a very small area
therefore there may be a great deal of variation both in
the dampness of the soil and the amount of sunlight
received, so that many different types of wild flowers,
such as foxgloves, primroses and fool's parsley brighten
the hedgerow community in the spring or summer.

ADAPTATION

Plants and animals have to adapt to their environment and way of life in order to survive. Cacti living in desert areas of America, where there is no rain for long periods, have fleshy stems which are able to take in large quantities of water after a sudden rainstorm and to store it for a long time. The mole, living underground, has very small eyes and strong shovel-like limbs for burrowing through the soil.

Many animals are *camouflaged* – coloured in such a way that they merge into their background and are difficult to see. The ground in heathland areas is frequently covered with fragments of bracken-fronds and

Nightjar

heather twigs, and several ground-nesting, heathland birds, such as the nightjar, have grey-brown, speckled plumage so that when sitting on their nests they are almost invisible. Similarly, the hind wings of a grayling butterfly are coloured in a way that resembles the light and dark greys of a piece of bark. When the butterfly settles on an old branch or a dried leaf, it seems to disappear!

Birds nesting amidst the sand and shingle of a seashore often have blotched or speckled light-coloured eggs that are very difficult to see. You can be within a few metres of a ringed plover's nest for an hour without finding it.

Grayling Butterfly

Peregrine Falcon

FOOD CHAINS

All animals and plants require food. Green plants are able to take in water and mineral salts from the soil, and a gas called carbon dioxide from the air. They use sunlight to build these into substances such as *carbohydrates* and *proteins*. This process is called *photosynthesis* which means 'building up using light'.

Animals are unable to make proteins and carbohydrates themselves and obtain their food direct from plants (such animals are called *herbivores* – 'plant eaters') or from other animals (*carnivores* – 'flesh eaters') that have themselves eaten plants. The various plants and animals linked in this way make up a *food chain*.

For example, heather is one of the commonest plants of the uplands of northern England and Scotland. The young shoots, flowers and seeds of the heather form important food sources for the red grouse, which is common in many moorland areas. Grouse in their turn may occasionally be taken by a bird of prey such as a peregrine falcon.

Grouse

FOOD WEBS

Simple food chains, such as those already described, seldom occur by themselves. In most habitats there are many different plants and animals; some creatures have several sources of food and may be eaten by any number of different predators. Food chains therefore join one another to form a *food web*.

Thus, in a freshwater pool or pond there are usually large numbers of minute plants, some so small that they

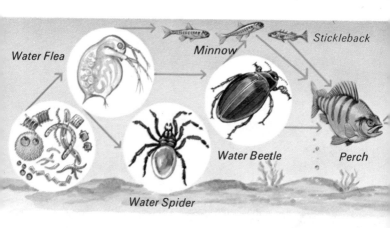

Water Flea
Minnow
Stickleback
Water Beetle
Perch
Water Spider

can only be seen with a microscope. These form the food of tiny animals such as water fleas. Water fleas are eaten by small fish like minnows which in their turn are taken by larger fish, for example, perch. Fish may also be eaten by birds like the kingfisher and heron. Water spiders and water beetles are examples of smaller predators. Other food chains are based on water weeds – duck, for instance, feed on water plants, and pike (predatory fish up to a metre (3 ft) in length) often take

Kingfisher

Heron

Duck

Pike

(*Note that only some of the possible food chains are shown.*)

ducklings as well as the young of other water-birds and quite large fish.

Frogs eat many of the smaller pond animals. They and the plant-eating watervoles also form part of the diet of pike, and in addition may occasionally be taken by a hungry heron.

Complex sets of food linkages such as these exist in almost every natural community.

THE ECOLOGICAL PYRAMID

There are usually smaller numbers of carnivores than there are of herbivores in a community; the number of *top carnivores* (animals that have no predators other than man) in any area may be very small indeed. A *pyramid of numbers* may be said to exist.

In a woodland habitat in summer, there are usually countless thousands of caterpillars and other small

Sparrow
Hawk

insects living on the leaves of trees and other plants. These creatures are eaten by small birds such as titmice and warblers, of which there may be several pairs to each hectare (2.47 acres) of woodland. Small birds form one of the sources of food of the sparrow hawk (the top carnivore) but there is normally only one pair of these birds of prey in quite a large area of woodland.

As the creatures that are high in the pyramid have to search a larger area for their food than those lower down they tend to be larger. Thus a ladybird is larger than the aphids (small plant-eating insects such as greenfly) on which it feeds, and a predatory mammal such as a stoat or weasel is several times the size of the field-mice and bank voles which it hunts.

PARASITES AND SAPROPHYTES

A *parasite* is an animal or plant that does not obtain food in the normal way but which lives within or upon another plant or animal (the *host*) and takes food from it.

Many mammals and birds, for example, have fleas and lice living amongst their fur or feathers and feeding on their blood.

Sometimes you will see threads of a light pinkish plant, known as dodder, entwined amongst the stems of plants such as heather. Dodder contains no green *chlorophyll* and so is not able to photosynthesize (see page 8). It takes its food through *suckers* that penetrate the stem of its host.

Mistletoe is an example of a *partial parasite*; it contains chlorophyll but also requires food from another plant. An apple tree is often the host.

The cuckoo is sometimes called a parasite as it lays its eggs in the nests of other birds instead of rearing its own young.

Where a parasite uses a plant or animal of importance to man as its host it may be a serious pest. Liver-flukes are little animals that live inside sheep and can make them ill. Sometimes wheat crops are spoilt by 'rust', a fungus that lives on the ears of wheat.

There are some plants that live on the decaying remains of other plants and animals: such plants are called *saprophytes*. Like parasitic plants, saprophytes are not able to carry out photosynthesis and do not contain green chlorophyll.

In autumn many fungi grow in woodlands and meadows; they obtain their food from dead leaves and other decaying material in the soil. The field mushroom is an example. Some fungi (moulds, toadstools, etc.) grow on dead timber, others live on dung or animal carcasses. The moulds that grow on stale bread and old cheese are also saprophytic fungi.

A few flowering plants such as the bird's nest orchis are also saprophytes.

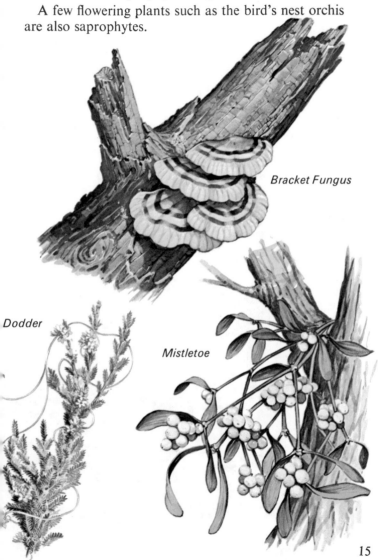

Bracket Fungus

Dodder

Mistletoe

SYMBIOSIS AND COMMENSALISM

Sometimes two different plants, or a plant and an animal, live together for their mutual advantage. This is *symbiosis*.

Lichens, for example, that grow on rocks and walls, are made up of a fungus and an *alga* (a simple green plant) living within it. The fungus protects the alga to some extent, and may be able to store water in dry periods, while the alga is able to photosynthesize and so provide food for the fungus. Other minute algae live in corals.

Commensalism is a less close association than symbiosis. It is a food-sharing relationship, but

Cladonia Lichen

sometimes one party is the provider, receiving little or nothing in return.

The hermit crab has no hard shell but lives in the abandoned shell of another creature such as a whelk. Quite frequently a sea anemone grows on this shell, and is able to eat leftover food that drifts upwards from the hermit crab's meals. Sometimes a worm shares the crab's borrowed home as well as its sources of food. Another example of commensalism is the association between a shark and the pilot fish that swims ahead of it feeding from the remains of its much larger partner's meals.

*Hermit Crab
with Sea Anemone*

OTHER EXAMPLES OF CO-OPERATION

Sometimes animals gain benefits other than food from a relationship with another animal or a plant.

In Africa birds called ox-peckers perch on the backs of large animals such as giraffes and cattle, and 'groom' them by removing tiresome insects. The ox-peckers also give warning of the approach of danger through their cries and disturbed flight.

One animal sometimes provides a home for another; there are, for example, defenceless fish that live unharmed amongst the stinging tentacles of jellyfish, and birds such as the wheatear sometimes nest in rabbit burrows.

Bumble bee on White Dead Nettle

Many flowering plants are *pollinated* by insects (pollination is the transfer of the powdery pollen grains from one part of a flower to another, or sometimes to a different flower, so that seeds may form). Some flowers are shaped to suit a particular insect. When a bumblebee alights on a white dead nettle and pushes its head into the flower in search of nectar, the pollen is smeared on to the bumblebee's back.

Seeds, once formed, may also be distributed by animals. Where the seed is surrounded by fleshy material (as in the case of hips and haws) birds eat and transport them. The *burrs* on plants such as burdock have hooks that may catch on to fur and feathers.

LAYERING

Communities are often made up of a series of *layers*. For example, in a woodland one can see the *canopy*, made up of the boughs of trees such as oak, beech or elm, 5-10 metres (16 ft – 32 ft) from the ground, a *shrub-layer* made up of hawthorn, elder or hazel shrubs 2-3 metres (6 ft 6 in– 9 ft 9 in) high, a *herb-layer* a metre (3 ft 3 in) or so from the ground as well as the *topsoil* and *subsoil*.

Different animals tend to live within each layer. Rooks may nest in the topmost branches, wood pigeons in the tangle of hawthorn beneath, and pheasants may lay their eggs in a hollow on the woodland floor.

Nevertheless important links exist between the layers. Winter-moth caterpillars feed on the tree-leaves in oak woods but crawl down the trunks to *pupate* (turn into chrysalids, the half-way stage between caterpillar and moth) in the soil.

Wood Pigeons

Rooks

Pheasant

AN OAK TREE AS A COMMUNITY

There are some 230 types of insects that live on oak trees. This number includes over 80 moths which have caterpillars that feed on oak leaves, as well as many types of flies and beetles. Winter-moth caterpillars may become particularly abundant with perhaps as many as 60,000 feeding on the leaves of one oak tree. Sometimes they destroy almost the entire leaf canopy of an oak.

Larva of Scalloped Oak Moth

Gall Wasp

Oak-gall

Larva of Vapourer Moth

Grey Squirrel

The leaf-feeders of the oak canopy provide food for many predators. These include small spiders, some of which are seldom found away from oak trees, as well as birds such as blue tits and wood warblers.

Other small creatures live only in acorns. Another group of insects that dwell on the oak tree is the gall-formers. There are several dozen gall-wasps which have grubs that live within the leaves and twigs of oak trees and cause the growth of *oak-galls* (the marble-like *oak-apple* is a typical example). Galls in their turn provide homes for several other insects, some of which feed on the gall-makers!

An oak tree thus supports a most elaborate food web. And it may also be the home of animals such as squirrels that build their *dreys* (nests) within its branches, and of owls that nest in hollow cavities within its trunk, but which seek some of their food elsewhere.

SUCCESSION I

Many plant communities gradually change with time, and the way in which one set of plants follows another is known as *succession*.

The first stage in a succession is known as a *pioneer community*. For example, there are relatively few plants that are able to live under the dry conditions of unstable sand dunes. Marram grass is often the only plant found growing in such places. The roots of this pioneer plant bind the sand together. As the sand dunes become more stable, other plants, such as heather, follow the marram, and provide a more complete plant cover. This heathland community will in its turn be invaded by shrubs and bushes (such as birch) and ultimately woodland will form.

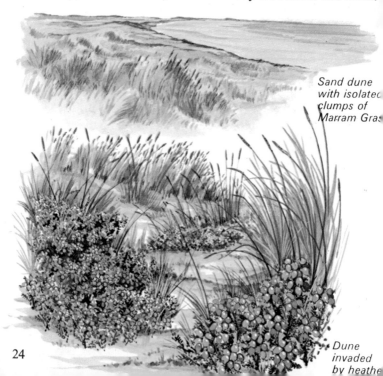

Sand dune with isolated clumps of Marram Grass

Dune invaded by heather

The whole process may take several hundred years.

The animal communities change along with the plants. Relatively few insects or other animals are able to live amidst the open sand dunes. Many more types inhabit the heathland that follows the dune community, and the woodland may support a great variety of insects, spiders, birds and other creatures.

Sometimes there is a series of sand dune ridges along a coast, each of a different age. The ridge nearest the sea will have been blown there by the wind most recently and is likely to support a pioneer community. Those a little inland will be clothed with heath, scrub or woodland. Parallel sets of dunes of this nature exist on the Lancashire coast near Formby and at Studland Heath in Dorset.

Birch woodland developing on heathland

SUCCESSION II

Changes also occur in a stretch of open water.

When a pool first appears – for example, when a gravel-pit is worked out and abandoned – water plants such as duckweeds, Canadian pondweed and water lily are the first to establish themselves. As time passes, however, silt is brought in from outside the pool and dead plant material accumulates on the pond bottom,

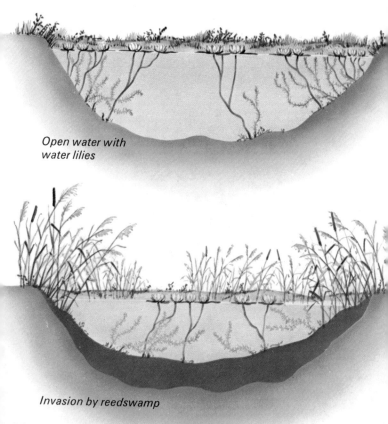

Open water with water lilies

Invasion by reedswamp

Depression filled with peat—
"carr" growth developing

so that the pool gradually gets shallower. Reeds then
invade round the edges, and in time the entire pool will
become overwhelmed by reedswamp. Eventually
the whole depression is filled with dark *peat* – dead plant
material.

A *carr*, or low tangled woodland with willow and
buckthorn, follows the reedswamp community, and if
the area continues to remain undisturbed, tall oak or ash
woodland often represents the last stage in the succession.

Very frequently, however, a succession is not allowed
to follow its full natural course. For example, a patch of
open water may be dredged before the filling-in process
is complete or, as in the Norfolk Broads area of East
Anglia, the reedbeds may be cut as a source of reed for
thatching.

A NATURAL EXPERIMENT

Ecological changes are sometimes much more rapid than those of succession described on the previous four pages.

One such change followed the arrival of the rabbit disease, *myxomatosis*, in Britain in 1953. By the end of 1955 almost all parts of England, Wales and Scotland were affected. Rabbits died in large numbers. Many plants, no longer grazed by hungry rabbits, were able to grow up and flower in a way that had not been possible before. In some cases open expanses of heather and grassland

Typical pasture before myxomatosis

were invaded by scrub. Because hares no longer had to compete for food with rabbits, they increased in numbers. Stoats and other predators were deprived of one of their main sources of food, so turned towards other prey – small birds for example – and became much less numerous. Some birds, such as the wheatear, were affected as they no longer had burrows in which to build their nests.

A change in the numbers of one type of animal or plant can thus quite rapidly affect the whole community.

The same pasture after myxomatosis showing changes in flora and fauna

ZONATION

Because of the twice daily rise and fall of the tides, conditions on a seashore vary widely between the different levels. At low water mark the rocks or sand are exposed to the air for relatively short periods at a time, while at the top of the beach, plants and animals are only covered by the sea for a few minutes around high water. Different communities of plants and animals can therefore be found at different levels on the beach. This arrangement of the communities into parallel bands or zones is known as *zonation*.

Serrated Wrack

Oar-weed

LOWER SHORE

On rocky coasts, ribbons of brown oar-weed up to two metres (6 ft 6 in) in length are often found in the lowermost zone. A little higher, low water reveals slippery masses of a seaweed called serrated wrack, which has jagged edges to its fronds. Higher still grows the bladder-wrack, with rounded *air-bladders* acting as floats. In the *splash zone*, seldom entirely covered by salt water, black and yellow lichens encrust the rocks.

Bladder Wrack

UPPER SHORE

COMPETITION AND THE BALANCE OF NATURE

A pair of song-thrushes may raise two broods a year, with five or six nestlings in each brood; every autumn an oak tree may produce many thousands of acorns. Yet the numbers of oak trees and thrushes in the countryside are not increasing. This is because animals and plants have to compete for food, water, light and space, and a great many do not survive to become adults. Numbers are therefore held in check.

A woodland of, say, five hectares (12.3 acres) can support a limited number of thrushes, voles, tawny owls and stoats. If, for a time, the number of voles increases beyond a certain point, there will not be enough food to go round, and some will starve or become diseased. Also the numbers of birds and beasts of prey (stoats, weasels, owls and hawks) will increase, and before long the number of voles will be reduced. This is called the *balance of nature*.

Tawny Owl with Vole

Sometimes man disrupts this balance. Farmers and gamekeepers from time to time shoot or poison stoats and owls, so that the numbers of mice and voles increase to a level where they eat so many nuts and acorns that few are left to grow up into trees to replace those that die or are felled.

FROM FOREST TO FARMLAND

Much of Britain was once covered by forest. Since the land was first farmed in the New Stone Age (about 4,500 years ago), the woodland has gradually been cleared, and farmland and grassland communities have extended over the face of the country. By the time of King William I's Domesday survey in 1086, the woodland had gone from much of the east and south of the country.

A cultivated field is a much more simple community than a woodland. Yet the ecology of farmland can be quite complex in spite of the increasing use of *insecticides* (poisons that kill insects) and *herbicides* (weed killers).

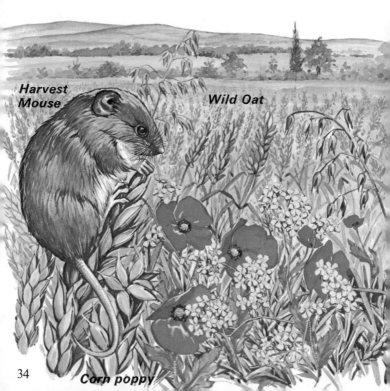

Harvest Mouse

Wild Oat

Corn poppy

The red corn poppy and the wild oat are still to be found in English cornfields. Several birds, such as the corn bunting, find cropland an attractive habitat.

There may be important ecological links between a field and hedgerow and rough ground communities nearby. Ladybirds sometimes move from the hedges to breed in cereal fields where they eat aphids (pests that feed on the sap of plants). Partridges eat a good deal of grain from the stubble left after harvest, but also require an area of scrub or a hedge bank in which to breed.

Corn Bunting

Partridge

MAN-MADE FORESTS

Over the centuries so much woodland was cleared that eventually Britain began to grow short of timber. In 1919 the *Forestry Commission* was formed and given the task of planting new forest. Several hundred thousand hectares (1 hectare = 2.47 acres) of land already carry tree crops. *Conifers* (cone-bearing trees) such as Scots and Corsican pine are widely planted, as they grow quickly. In places the Commission has planted *deciduous* trees (trees which lose their leaves in the winter, such as oak and beech) to add variety to the landscape.

Plantations containing only one kind of tree tend to provide homes for fewer other plants and animals than natural woodland. Birds such as titmice feed amongst the pine branches. Fungi grow well amongst the needles on the ground of conifer plantations in the autumn. Deer and grey squirrels live in many Commission woodlands and sometimes damage young trees. When these animals become too numerous they are controlled by shooting.

Pine forest with felled logs   *Observation tower*

The first task of the Forestry Commission is to provide timber for industry. Today, however, the forester makes every effort to beautify the landscape and to protect wild life. He also provides opportunities for outdoor activities for young people; for example by making picnic areas and camp-sites available and laying out *nature trails* (walks through the woodland, with items of interest clearly labelled and explained). Sometimes observation towers are built so that visitors can watch deer and other animals. Amongst the larger Commission forests are Thetford Forest in eastern England, Kielder in Northumbria and the Queen Elizabeth Forest Park in Scotland.

Fallow deer (opposite)

CONSERVATION

Conservation is the wise use of land, water and the plants and animals that they support.

Thus the replanting of forests at the same rate that they are felled, and the use of the forests for wildlife protection and outdoor activities as well as for timber growing, are examples of conservation.

Alternate strip ploughing

The planting of the same crops on farmland year after year exhausts the soil and renders it infertile. Soil conservation involves *crop rotation*, so that land does not bear the same crop more than once in five or six years, giving it time to recover its fertility. *Soil-building crops* such as clover are planted to enrich the soil. In America in the 1920s and 1930s when croplands were left bare, the topsoil was blown away. Now rows of trees are planted as windbreaks, and *cover crops* are used so that the soil is not left exposed for long periods. Contour ploughing and strip cropping also tend to prevent the removal of the soil.

If any animals – red deer, fish, whales, grouse – are taken in great numbers at one time, few are left to breed. Wildlife conservation does not seek to prevent shooting, fishing or whaling, but tries to arrange things so that only a limited number of animals are taken each year. Fishing and shooting are not allowed in the breeding season, to give animals, birds and fish the chance to reproduce without disturbance.

NATURE RESERVES

As so much of the land is used intensively by man, it is important that examples of natural and nearly natural communities should be carefully preserved for scientific study and education. Also, increasing numbers of people enjoy such activities as bird watching and wildlife photography.

In Britain the Nature Conservancy, the National Trust, the Royal Society for the Protection of Birds and the County Naturalists' Trusts are amongst the bodies that have set up Nature Reserves for these purposes.

Examples of Nature Reserves include the Farne Islands off the Northumbrian coast where there are large colonies of sea-birds such as guillemot and kittiwake and where seals breed; the wild moorlands at Moor House in the northern Pennines; and the woods, heaths and marshes at Minsmere in Suffolk.

Nature Reserves are carefully managed so as to provide as wide a range of habitats as possible. Thus overgrown pools are cleaned out to make stretches of open water for duck, and areas of heathland may be burnt or cut to prevent invasion by scrub. Nest-boxes are often provided to increase the numbers of breeding birds.

NATIONAL PARKS

National Parks are areas of outstanding natural beauty that are set aside for outdoor activities, and where the landscape is carefully protected.

In Britain, Dartmoor, the Derbyshire Peak District, North Wales, the Yorkshire Dales and the Lake District are all National Park areas. Rambling, canoeing, climbing, and the study of natural history are encouraged, and unsightly building and quarrying are, as far as

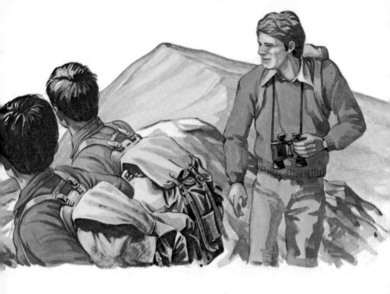

possible, prevented. Activities such as farming and forestry are allowed to continue.

In the African countries and the USA, the National Parks are large areas, in some cases including many thousands of hectares that are kept, as far as possible, in their natural state. Agriculture, hunting, mining and building are not allowed.

African parks (the Serengeti Plains in Tanzania and the Kruger Park in the Transvaal, for example) are best known for the vast herds of animals such as antelopes and zebra, which, followed by prides of lions and other predators, wander over the grassland. In the USA hundreds of thousands of people visit the National Parks each year to admire such magnificent spectacles as the Grand Canyon in Arizona, the mountain and forest scenery of Yellowstone in Montana, and Yosemite in California.

POLLUTION I

Pollution is loss of purity and contamination of any form of life. There are many types of chemical which, when added to air, water or soil (whether by accident or on purpose) can have a harmful effect on plants and animals.

Insecticides and herbicides (see page 34) are widely used by farmers. Unfortunately some of these chemicals are very persistent – they do not 'break down' or decay in nature. One result of this is that they tend to be passed along food chains. A caterpillar containing a very tiny quantity of a poison may be eaten by a small bird and this, in its turn, may be taken by a bird of prey. Both owls and peregrine falcons have been found with very large amounts of certain insecticides in their bodies. Often their eggs have not hatched, so that their numbers have declined. This may imbalance a whole community of plants and animals.

Chemicals used on farmland are often washed out of soils into streams and rivers where they contaminate the fish. Fish-eating birds such as the kingfisher and certain predaceous fish have suffered in a similar way to the owl and the peregrine falcon. Sometimes a drum that contained a poisonous chemical is left not quite empty in a drainage ditch, so that the water may be poisoned for many kilometres downstream.

POLLUTION II

Factories sometimes release poisonous waste into rivers, or the sea, but laws are being passed to stop this. The control of ships at sea is more difficult. Sometimes oil is released deliberately or when a ship is damaged. When an oil tanker, the *Torrey Canyon*, foundered on rocks off the Cornish coast in March, 1967, many thousands of tonnes of crude oil were released. Thousands of sea-birds were 'oiled', became unable to fly, and died. Shellfish and other seashore creatures along the coasts of south-west England and northern France were also killed by this pollution.

*Atmospheric pollution
in an industrial city*

The air is also often polluted. The burning of petrol and coal releases gases such as sulphur dioxide into the air. These are poisonous to many plants and animals. Where the air is pure, away from cities for example, in western Scotland and Ireland, lichens of many types cover the branches of trees and the rocks, but only a few hardy types survive in large towns.

The passing of laws to reduce air pollution, as well as making our country cleaner to live in, is thus an important part of conservation.

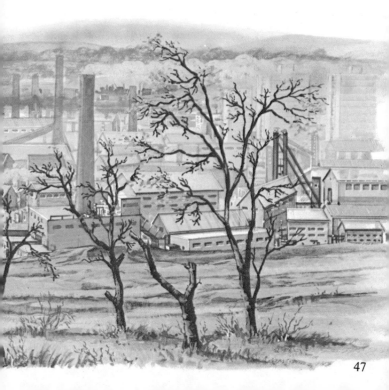

ROADSIDES AND MOTORWAYS

Roadside verges, although they are artificial habitats, are frequently important refuges for wild flowers and certain types of wild life. In many areas, the grassy strips along country roads are all that remains of grassland and meadow habitats that have been ploughed up elsewhere. Thus in Suffolk and Cambridgeshire, in eastern England, plants such as certain types of orchis, broom-rape and yellow-wort can still be found growing along roadsides although they have disappeared from nearby farmlands. Often well over a hundred species of plants can be found growing along a five kilometre (3 mile) length of verge. In summer several species of butterflies may be seen feeding from the flowers along such a stretch.

Where the verge is bordered by a hedge and a ditch, it may provide a home for even more plants and animals

Small birds such as chaffinches, and mammals such as hedgehogs, that live in the hedgerows, may be killed by passing vehicles. Carrion crows are frequently seen eating creatures that have perished in this way.

A kilometre (⅝ mile) of motorway requires about five hectares (12.3 acres) of land, of which forty per cent is verge. Although they are not often disturbed by visitors, such areas are much affected by noise and fumes – many plants and animals living near motorways have been found to have lead and other poisons from exhaust fumes in their bodies. Voles and mice may live on motorway verge areas in quite large numbers. Because they can be easily seen in the short grass these animals provide food for kestrels which have become quite a familiar sight along Britain's motorways.

ECOLOGY IN TOWNS AND CITIES

Although the protection of natural communities in Nature Reserves and National Parks is most important, there are many types of plants and animals which have successfully adapted their way of life to man-made habitats.

Flowers such as rosebay willow-herb, dandelion and ragwort thrive in well-drained areas such as railway yards, docksides and building sites. In the hearts of many large cities, a few specimens of lichens and mosses are usually to be found growing on roofs and walls.

Willow Herb

Herring Gull

Jackdaw

Starling

Dandelion

Common Ragwort

Many animals eat food left by man; quite complex food-webs exist in and around rubbish dumps. Foxes, rats, and herring gulls are amongst the animals found in such places. Birds such as starlings, jackdaws, and house sparrows nest in and around buildings. Birds of prey are sometimes found nesting close to the centre of cities, using large office-blocks as though they were cliffs. They feed on rats, mice and pigeons.

Dock

INDEX OF NATURE'S ROUNDABOUT